"And let the peace of Christ rule in your hearts, to which indeed you were called in one body; and be thankful."
Colossians 3:15 RSV

To Erik

PAUL
A Change of Heart
Retold by Anne de Graaf
Illustrated by José Pérez Montero
©Copyright 1990 by Scandinavia Publishing House
Nørregade 32, DK-1165 Copenhagen K

English-language edition published through
special arrangement with Scandinavia by
Wm. B. Eerdmans Publishing Co.,
255 Jefferson Ave. S.E., Grand Rapids, Michigan 49503
All rights reserved
Printed in Hong Kong

ISBN 0-8028-5034-0

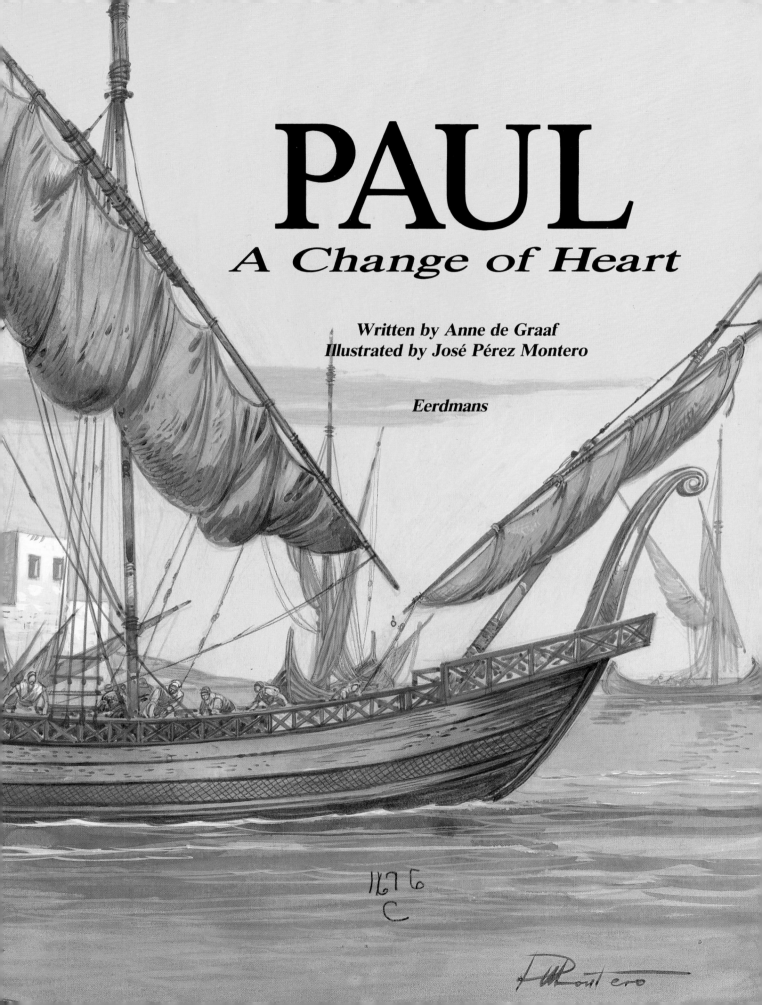

PAUL
A Change of Heart

Written by Anne de Graaf
Illustrated by José Pérez Montero

Eerdmans

Saul's anger rose in him like a fire. "Stephen has gone too far!" he shook with rage.

Stephen stood in the middle of a great hall. All around him, religious leaders shook their fists. Stephen lifted his hands up high. He reached for something none of them could see.

"Look!" Stephen pointed. "The heavens are opening up. There is Jesus, standing next to God!"

"Enough!" Saul shouted.

"Stone him!"

"We don't want to hear anymore!" the religious leaders cried out.

"Don't listen!" Saul told the rest. They covered their ears and rushed at Stephen.

Guards grabbed the prisoner and dragged him out of the city. A mob of angry, yelling people followed. The religious leaders, including Saul, told the people what had happened.

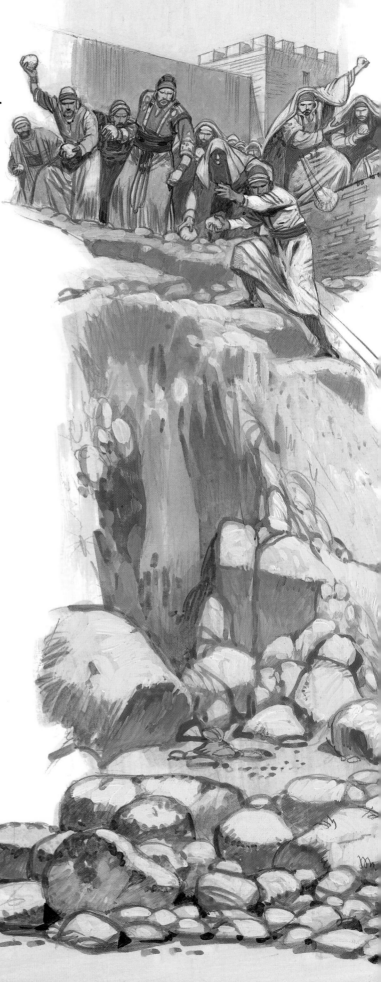

"He says Jesus was the Son of God. He talks as if He were His best friend!"

"He made fun of God!"

As they threw Stephen down the hill, they began stoning him. Saul shouted with the rest, "Kill him before he says anything more against God."

Stephen steadied himself with one hand while the other reached toward heaven. "Lord Jesus!" Stephen said. "Take me, please!"

"Don't listen! He'll poison your minds!" Saul roared.

Stephen's last words were, "Lord, don't hold this against them!" Then Stephen said no more. He had gone to heaven. There he would never again feel the sharp pain of stones.

The crowd threw more rocks until the crumpled body lay half buried. Then, slowly, they backed away, breathing hard. Some shook their heads, "He deserved worse."

A mother pulled her child away. "I want to see, I want to see!" the boy cried.

"There's nothing to see," his mother mumbled.

Saul walked with the other religious leaders back to the Temple. As he came alongside the chief priest, he said to the important man, "That was just the beginning. From now on we wage war against the followers of Jesus. Who do they think they are? Again and again they break the Law."

Soon Saul had driven most of the Christians out of Jerusalem. Then he went to the high priest. "If you would give the word, I could make sure these followers of Jesus are stamped out. With a letter from you, I could travel to Damascus and hunt them down." He paused, letting his words sink in.

"I'll bring them back bound to Jerusalem, then throw them into prison. We can punish them as we did Stephen. No one, not one more person than I can help will have to hear anymore about Jesus. His name will be wiped out, His memory forgotten."

So important was Saul's mission that the high priest not only gave him the letter he had asked for, but a special guard as well. Saul rode off toward Damascus. He believed in his heart he was doing the right thing.

What is right and what is wrong? Sometimes our hearts are the only voices which tell us. And sometimes it takes a change of heart before we can learn the truth. This is what happened to Saul. Only then could he grasp what was truly right and what was wrong.

Saul and his guard galloped through the desert. By noon they were within sight of the great city, Damascus. And then, suddenly, a light flashed around Saul.

"Agh!" he screamed and threw his hands up to protect his eyes. His horse reared and Saul tumbled to the ground. He saw nothing. The dazzling light had blinded him!

"Saul! Saul!" he heard a Voice. "Why do you keep hurting Me so much?"

The guards riding with Saul also saw the light. Mouths open, they heard the sound, but could not understand it. Saul knew what the Voice was saying, though. "Who are You?" he cried.

"I am Jesus. I am the One you have been hunting down and hurting."

Saul felt a knife cut into his heart. He had been wrong! All this time, he had wanted so badly to follow the rules. But he had ended up hurting the very Lord he served! The knife of shame twisted as Saul felt his heart change.

"What," he gasped. "What can I do? Lord, tell me what I should do!"

"Get up and go on into Damascus," the Voice said. "There you will be told about My plan for your life." Saul nodded. Then the light was gone.

Silence. Saul heard only the desert wind and the stamp of his horse. He called out to the guards, "Damascus. Take me to Damascus. That's where I must go. Lead me there, will you please?"

Step by step the guards led the blinded Saul into Damascus. There he did not eat or drink anything for three days. Then the Lord sent one of His followers to make Saul better.

And so Saul joined the very followers of Jesus he had sworn to kill. God had changed Saul's heart. Now Saul knew, without a doubt, Jesus was the right Way, the only Way to God.

It was not easy for the Christians to accept Saul as one of their own. Not so long ago he had hunted them down. Now he wanted to come to their prayer meetings.

The followers of Jesus listened to Saul preach, "Jesus is the Christ! He really is the Son of God and He's alive today!"

The religious leaders in Damascus did not like this at all! One of their very own had turned against them. No matter how they

argued, though, Saul was able to outwit them. Again and again he proved Jesus is the Son of God. Jesus' Holy Spirit gave Saul the right words.

The Christians in Damascus had no choice. "Just listen to him. God has turned an enemy into a friend."

But the religious leaders said, "He's changed from a friend into an enemy! We must kill Saul before he causes more trouble!"

Word of the plot reached the Christians. "Hurry, Saul, we must get you out of Damascus. These religious leaders are serious."

"I know,"Saul sighed. "I used to be one of them."

That night Saul's new friends led him up dark stairs, all the way to the top of the city walls. "They're watching the gates. No one will expect you to escape this way."

Three men held a huge basket as Saul climbed in. "We'll pray for you!"

Saul and a friend of his named Barnabas traveled from one village to another. "Have you heard?" they asked people wherever they went. "God sent His only Son. His name is Jesus. If you ask Him to, He will forgive all the bad things you've done. You can start over. Believe in Jesus! Ask Him to come live in your hearts. Ask Him today!"

It was during this time that Saul changed his name to Paul. That was the Roman way of saying his name. So now, whenever the two men entered a village people said, "Paul! Barnabas! Please come teach us what you know. We've heard a little, but want to know more."

One of the towns Paul and Barnabas visited was called Lystra. There, Paul and Barnabas taught the people. "Believe in Jesus. He can help you with your problems!"

One day a very sick man came to Paul. This man had never been able to walk! As he listened to Paul talk about Jesus, he thought, "Yes, I believe in Jesus. Yes!"

Paul looked at the man and saw he was trusting Jesus. He prayed that God might help the man. Then Paul said loudly, "Stand up on your feet."

The man jumped up. He began to walk! The crowd cried, "Paul is a god!"

"So is Barnabas!"

"No! No!" Paul and Barnabas shouted. This was the last thing they wanted. They had come to point people toward Jesus, not themselves.

The crowd finally calmed down. But a few days later, something terrible happened. This same crowd who had thought Paul and Barnabas were so wonderful, suddenly turned against them.

The religious leaders wanted very much to cause trouble for Paul and Barnabas. They had secretly told the people, "Paul doesn't know what he's talking about. Don't listen to him. He thinks Jesus is the Son of God. He says God loves everyone. That's crazy!"

The people did not think for themselves. They did not let their own hearts choose what was right and what was wrong. Instead they let the religious leaders choose for them.

"Kill Paul!"

"Throw rocks at him until he dies!"

"Stone the troublemaker!"

So many angry people. They had hardened their hearts against Paul's message from Jesus. They yelled and screamed. yet Paul stood, a hero for Jesus.

When the sharp rocks dug into his back, his legs, his face, he sank to his knees. Paul knew what Stephen had felt. The pain dug deep, until finally, Paul could feel no more.

Paul's body lay still. The mob had dragged him out of the city. They thought he was dead.

A boy stood over the bruised and bleeding body. He stared, tears streaming down his face. "Is Paul dead?" he whispered.

Barnabas and a few others had come to bury Paul's body. Barnabas was just about to answer the boy, when he saw Paul move. "No, Timothy, he's not!" Barnabas shouted. "Look everyone, it's a miracle!" He helped Paul to his feet.

The others could not believe their eyes. Surely Paul had died. Yet there he was, standing up.... and walking. "Paul, Oh Paul!" they cried. Young Timothy hugged him with the rest.

As Paul walked back into the city, he put his arm around Timothy. He had often seen Timothy listening when he talked about Jesus. The boy never said much, but Paul could tell by his eyes that every word had touched Timothy's heart. Paul looked down at the boy.

"Lord," he asked. "I wonder if someday I could have a son like this one."

At that same moment, Timothy prayed, "Please, Jesus, let me grow up to be like Paul. I want to learn from him."

Jesus answered both their prayers. About a year later Paul came back to Lystra. This time he traveled with a friend called Silas.

Paul asked Timothy to come with him and Silas as they went to different villages.

Timothy was only too happy to say yes. His heart danced as day after day, month after month, the two became like father and son.

Day after day after day, Paul and his friends sailed from one port to the next. Then they walked down the dusty Roman roads and visited as many villages as they could. Wherever they went, Paul, Silas and Timothy talked about Jesus. In many places the people listened. God opened their hearts so that they believed in Jesus.

Paul helped set up churches by choosing leaders for the groups of Christians. He taught them to share money with the poor. He helped them feel strong when other people wanted to hurt them for believing in Jesus.

For almost eight years Paul traveled by boat and on foot, from country to country. Often he went back to places where the people needed him most. He even managed to be in two places at once. He did this by writing letters to the groups of Christians he could not visit. In this way Paul showed that he still cared and was praying for them.

As Paul traveled, he sometimes stayed with friends. Sometimes he had nowhere to stay and made tents so he could buy food. He sometimes left Silas or Timothy behind to help solve problems certain groups were having.

15

Paul and Silas were always on the move. Over and over again they were forced to leave places by the religious leaders. It did not matter that he had once been one of them. Everywhere Paul went, they found reasons to arrest Paul.

In a town called Philippi the religious leaders told a huge mob to attack Paul and Silas. They beat them with sticks and threw them into prison. Paul and Silas lay on the cold stone floor, their hands chained. The guards had locked their feet between huge blocks of wood. They could not move at all! What do you think they did?

They sang songs! Paul and Silas were happy. They knew that Jesus takes very special care of people who are hurt because they believe in Him. He stands right by them and comforts them so much, they feel joyful enough to sing. And that is just what Paul did.

"We love Jesus, praise His name. Jesus, Jesus, thank You for standing by us!" On into the night the two men sang. They sang their hearts out while all the other prisoners listened.

Around midnight something very strange happened. A terrible roar rocked the prison! The earthquake shook the prison so hard, all the cell doors came flying open! Then the chains binding the prisoners unlocked. God had set the prisoners free!

When the jailer saw this, he trembled with fear. "Who are you?" he asked. He fell down at Paul's feet. "Please," he begged. "Tell me what has happened here tonight. I overheard you talking to the other prisoners about being saved. What does that mean? What do I have to do to be saved?"

Paul looked at Silas. They knew that this man's change of heart was an even greater miracle than the earthquake. Paul smiled at the frightened jailer. "Believe in the Lord Jesus and you will be saved. So will your family."

The jailer did believe. He took Silas and Paul that very night to his home. There he washed their sores and wounds, then gave them food to eat. Then the jailer and his family prayed to Jesus and asked Him into their hearts.

Paul wished that everyone they spoke to would believe as the jailer and his family had. When a group of Paul's enemies started chasing him from one village to the next, Paul hardly had time to teach anymore.

"There must be a way we can talk to more people about Jesus," Paul said to Silas.

"You could leave alone and cross the sea to Athens," Silas said. "That way Timothy and I could finish what you've started here. And you would be safe."

"Yes," Paul said. "That's a good idea. I can't be wasting so much time running and hiding. I don't like us splitting up, but maybe it's the only way. We must talk to more people about Jesus."

So once again, Paul sailed away. This time he traveled to Athens, a very old Greek city. There, the people prayed to many different gods. The Greeks had gods of the sun and moon and sea and war and peace and love and hate and rocks and fire and anything else you could think of.

"There is only one God!" Paul told them. Some of the Greeks listened and wanted to know more.

"You Greeks have made up gods to everything," Paul said. "Why, you even have a temple for the Unknown God. Well that's my God. And He's the only one you need to have. This God sent His Son Jesus. Let me tell you about Him...."

So Paul taught the Greeks. But many of them did not believe Paul. "Only one God? Ha ha! Paul is crazy! Don't listen to him!"

"I have better things to do then talk to people who won't hear me," Paul said. Together with the Greeks who did believe him, Paul set off to visit other islands in the area.

By sea and on foot, Paul traveled. Everywhere he went, Paul told people about Jesus. It was the most important news he could give them.

Greece was not the only place where Paul ran into people who believed in other gods. In Ephesus, part of the country we now call Turkey, Paul met people who believed in a god named Diana. They had built many statues and temples to Diana.

When Paul arrived in Ephesus, he liked it right away. There, many people wanted to hear his Good News about Jesus. They made Paul feel welcome. "Please teach us more about what all this means," they asked.

Paul stayed in Ephesus for two years. During that time, many, many people heard Paul speak. God helped them believe by giving Paul the power to make sick people better. Sometimes all Paul had to do was touch them and pray, and they would be healed!

There was one group of people, though, who did not like Paul. These were the people who wanted to worship Diana, rather than the one God. Some of these men had become rich by selling silver statues of Diana to the people.

"Thanks to Paul, we're not making as much money anymore," they complained.

"Yes, Paul has ruined our business by getting the people to believe in Jesus. Now no one wants to buy our statues!"

"Let's get rid of Paul!" The more these men shouted and grumbled, the angrier they became. "Let's go find Paul! We'll teach him a lesson!"

The mob went to the place where Paul taught the people. They yelled at him and started throwing rocks. "There he is! Stop the troublemaker!" they screamed.

Finally an official stopped the riot. No one was badly hurt.

Soon after this Paul left Ephesus. But the group of believers he left behind was one of the strongest in the area. They had learned the hard lesson that there is no middle road. Either you believe in Jesus or you don't.

Later Paul would write the Ephesians, helping his good friends there to grow even closer to God.

These letters by Paul were very important. Even with the help of friends like Timothy and Silas, Paul could not be everywhere at once. Paul's letters helped the people who had heard him and believed, to follow the Way.

"The Way" is living a life the way Jesus wants us to. Following the Way means loving enemies, praying to Jesus, and starting over whenever we make mistakes. Most of all, it means loving God more than anyone or anything else.

Paul made this clear in his letters. Often he and Timothy would ride from village to village. Whenever they spoke to people about Jesus, it was as if they were planting seeds of truth in their hearts.

When Paul had to leave new friends, he sent them letters. These letters acted as water for the seeds. The words were read and reread by many of the believers. God used these letters to help the seeds of truth grow into rich flowers of faith.

Men and women, children, the rich and the poor, everyone who wanted to believe,

did. Inside them all there grew this feeling that yes, of course, Jesus really is the Son of God!

This is the Way. The more people Paul and Timothy and the other followers of Jesus spoke with, the more believed. And just as the wind spreads the seeds of a flower so more flowers can grow, so, too, the followers of Jesus spread the Way to more and more and more people.

Soon the seeds of truth were scattering not just from one village to the next, but from country to country. Whole nations were hearing the Good News Paul and the other believers were talking about.

The special thing about Paul's letters is that they continue to spread seeds even today. Christians all over the world can read the words Paul wrote then to his friends. Reading Paul's letters is almost as good as having Paul and Timothy ride up to our house and talk to us in person! Now, as then, we can almost see the two of them, hear the hoofbeats, and feel the excitement.

Even when Paul's enemies were hunting him down, especially in the hard times, Paul's friends knew his words were important. Wherever Paul went, he warned the people about the religious leaders.

"They're lying," he told the people. "I know. For years I tried to be good enough by following the rules. I couldn't do it. My heart wanted so much to serve God. But I was blind. Now I can see. Jesus really is the Son of God!"

The religious leaders shook their fists at Paul. "He can't call us liars! Kill the traitor!"

The most dangerous place of all was Jerusalem, Paul's former home. Paul knew this. But he also knew Jesus was on his side. After so many years, Paul finally made his last trip through the countryside. He said good-bye to all his friends at the different churches. He knew he had to go to Jerusalem, no matter how dangerous it was.

Once Paul reached Jerusalem, it did not take his enemies long to spring their trap. The religious leaders lied to a mob of people who became so angry, they tried to kill Paul.

"There he is! Grab him!" The crowd went crazy with hatred. Paul's friends tried to protect him, but it was no good. The crowd dragged Paul out of the Temple.

"Stop this! Back away!"

"It's the Roman soldiers!" The crowd stopped beating Paul.

"What's this man done? Leave him alone!" The Roman captain had heard there was a riot in the city. He had sent soldiers to stop the fighting. Now he grabbed Paul. "Put this man in chains until we can find out what he's done," he ordered his men.

Then he asked why the crowd wanted to kill Paul. Some people said one thing. Others said something else. "Let us have him! We will give him what he deserves!" The crowd pushed against the Roman soldiers.

"No, you can't have him. We'll take the prisoner back with us," the captain ordered. The mob pressed so hard, though, that the soldiers had to carry Paul to keep him from being torn apart.

Once he was safely out of the crowd's reach, Paul asked twice if he could go back and talk to the religious leaders. "Please, I'm not a criminal. Let me talk to the people," he begged the captain.

Both times the crowd went wild with hatred. Finally, the Roman captain put him into prison. He told Paul, "I don't know who you are. I will punish you, though, until you tell me what you've done wrong."

Paul said, "I am a Roman. You cannot beat me without a trial."

These words, "I am a Roman," were very powerful. Paul was right. No one could put him into prison without a trial, not if he was a Roman. The Roman captain knew Paul was right. But he also knew that if he let Paul free, his own people would kill him. Once again he let Paul speak to the religious leaders. For the third time they screamed for Paul's death. This time the Roman captain put him back into prison, for his own good.

Paul had felt the Lord standing by him all this time. Jesus' own Holy Spirit had spoken through Paul, trying to reach the religious leaders. But their hearts were closed. Even Jesus cannot break through a heart which does not want to change.

That night, as Paul slept on the cold, stone floor, he saw the Lord standing right next to him! "Be brave, Paul," Jesus told him. "You've done the right thing, telling the people of Jerusalem about Me. Now you must do the same in Rome."

The next morning Paul woke up feeling the peace of God in his heart. "I'll follow You, Jesus, no matter what," he prayed. Paul was ready to do battle.

It was a good thing, too. That same night, forty of Paul's enemies had plotted how they would ambush Paul the next time he was allowed to speak to the people. Luckily, Paul's nephew heard about the plan and told the Roman captain.

"Get me two hundred men," he ordered a guard. Then he called for Paul and told him about the plot. "I'm not going to take any chances with you. You'll leave tonight under heavy guard. My men will see you to Caesarea. Then you'll be King Agrippa's problem."

Paul escaped on horseback, protected by the Romans from his very own people. But would he ever really be free again?

In Caesarea the Romans kept Paul prisoner for two years. Three different times he went to trial. Paul told his story to two Roman governors, as well as the king.

Even the powerful King Agrippa thought Paul made good sense. He saw no reason to keep him prisoner. He did not want to make the religious leaders angry, though. So, just like the others, King Agrippa did not let Paul go free.

Finally Paul told them, "I am a Roman. That means I can go to Rome and tell the emperor himself how I have done nothing wrong. Take me to Caesar!"

The Romans had no choice. They did as Paul asked. They put him on a ship bound for Rome. Now finally, he was going to the place where Jesus had told Paul he must go.

An armed guard, together with some of Paul's other friends, went with him. The voyage took several months since they kept running into bad weather.

Finally a terrible storm blew the ship up and down, around and around, as if it were a toy boat. The wind howled and the rain slashed the decks! All the crew thought, "This is the worst storm ever. We're all going to die!"

For two long, horrible weeks the hurricane tossed the ship back and forth. It was so dark, no one could even tell when it was night and when it was day!

Finally, Paul told the men, "You must eat. Stay brave. God has shown me that none of us will die, but you must be strong enough to swim!"

Paul was right. When the ship finally did sink, it was just off the shore of an island. Every one of the crew, together with Paul and his guards, swam to safety.

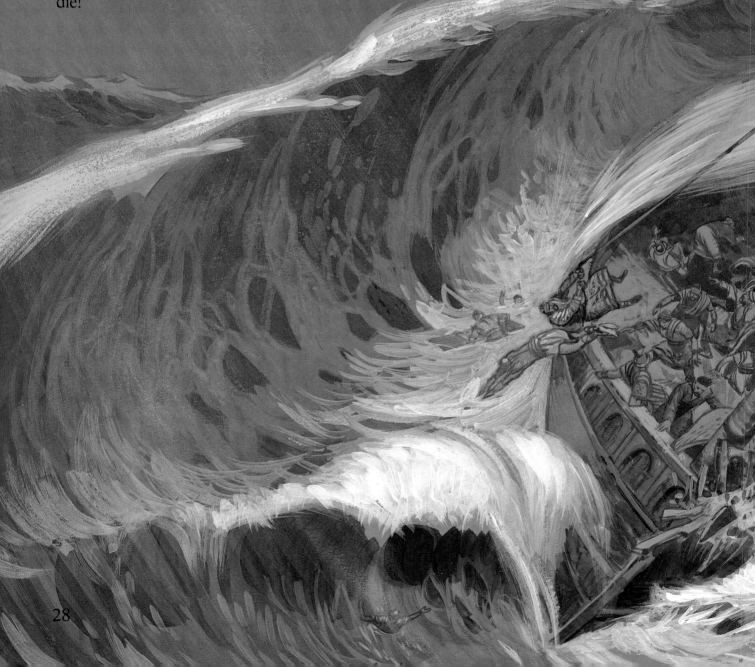

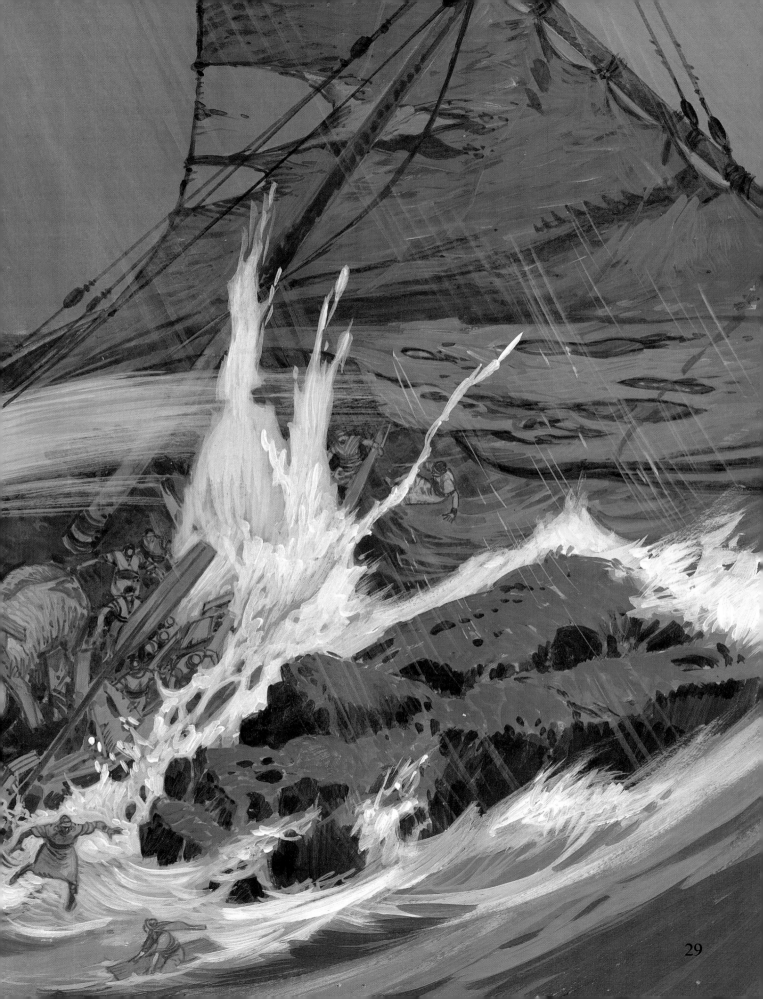

Safe at last, it did not take long to find another ship headed for Rome. By the time they finally did arrive in Rome, the captain of the guard had seen many times over what a good and honest man Paul was. Paul had bravely led them through their adventures.

Now the captain ordered, "If he must have a guard, all right. But let Paul go where he wants." The other believers welcomed Paul, together with the guard who followed him everywhere.

Paul's battle was not yet over. Paul spoke to the religious leaders. He talked to the important Romans who came to visit him. But no one wanted to anger the religious leaders in Jerusalem by giving Paul his freedom.

For several years Paul was free to live outside the prison. Many people came to hear Paul. He wrote more letters to his friends. But always, there was a Roman soldier standing guard over him.

Just when Paul seemed to have found a little bit of freedom, it was taken away from him again. One last time, Paul's enemies had him thrown into prison. There, Paul spent his last years, this time chained to his guard. In jail, he kept writing letters to the friends he had made during his long years of wandering. Up to the very end, Paul never stopped telling people about Jesus.

Just before he was killed, Paul wrote his young friend, Timothy, "How I long to see you. I can still remember how you cried when we last said good-bye. My son, please come and visit soon. I know the end is near. I am ready. I have fought the good fight, I have finished the race."

When Paul died, he left behind the stones of hatred and fear which had so often been thrown at him. He went to heaven. There he joined Stephen and all the many others who have chosen to let Jesus change their hearts.

You can find the story of Paul in the New Testament Book of Acts, chapters 9-28. Some of the letters Paul wrote are in the Bible. He wrote to the Romans, Corinthians, Galatians, Ephesians, Philippians, Colossians and Thessalonians, as well as to Timothy, Titus and Philemon.